THE EVOLUTION
OF AFRICA'S MAJOR NATIONS

Mozambique

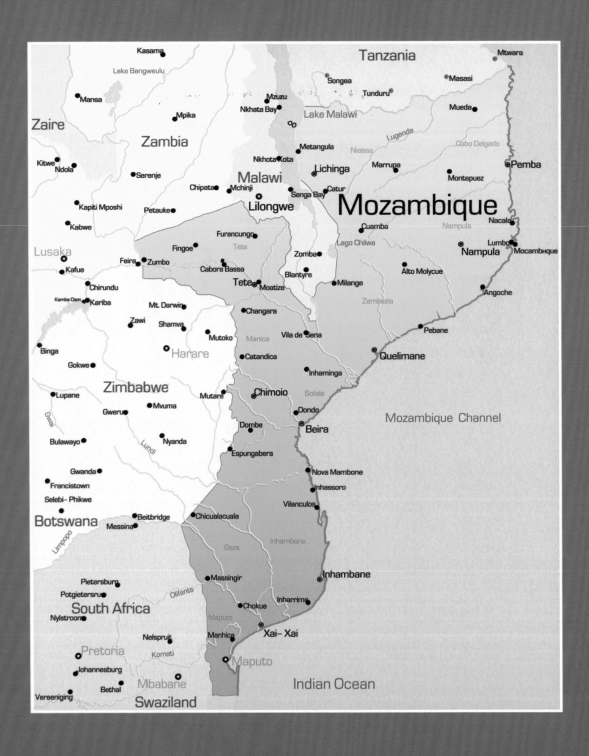

THE EVOLUTION
OF AFRICA'S MAJOR NATIONS

Mozambique

Tanya Mulroy

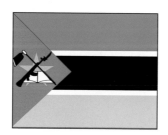

Mason Crest
Philadelphia

J

Mason Crest
370 Reed Road
Broomall, PA 19008
www.masoncrest.com

COUNTRIES
MOZAMBIQUE

CPSIA Compliance Information: Batch #EAMN2013-17. For further information,
contact Mason Crest at 1-866-MCP-Book.

First printing

1 3 5 7 9 8 6 4 2

Library of Congress Cataloging-in-Publication Data

Mulroy, Tanya.
  Mozambique / Tanya Mulroy.
     p. cm. — (Evolution of Africa's major nations.)
  Includes bibliographical references and index.
  ISBN 978-1-4222-2182-2 (hardcover)
  ISBN 978-1-4222-2210-2 (pbk.)
  ISBN 978-1-4222-9423-9 (ebooks)
  1. Mozambique—Juvenile literature. I. Title. II. Series: Evolution of Africa's major nations.
  DT3299.M85 2012
  967.9—dc22
                          2011018504

Africa: Facts and Figures
The African Union
Algeria
Angola
Botswana
Burundi
Cameroon
Democratic Republic
  of the Congo

Egypt
Ethiopia
Ghana
Ivory Coast
Kenya
Liberia
Libya
Morocco
Mozambique

Nigeria
Rwanda
Senegal
Sierra Leone
South Africa
Sudan
Tanzania
Uganda
Zimbabwe

Table of Contents

Africa: Progress, Problems, and Promise

Robert I. Rotberg

Africa is the cradle of humankind, but for millennia it was off the familiar, beaten path of global commerce and discovery. Its many peoples therefore developed largely apart from the diffusion of modern knowledge and the spread of technological innovation until the 17th through 19th centuries. With the coming to Africa of the book, the wheel, the hoe, and the modern rifle and cannon, foreigners also brought the vastly destructive transatlantic slave trade, oppression, discrimination, and onerous colonial rule. Emerging from that crucible of European rule, Africans created nationalistic movements and then claimed their numerous national independences in the 1960s. The result is the world's largest continental assembly of new countries.

There are 53 members of the African Union, a regional political grouping, and 48 of those nations lie south of the Sahara. Fifteen of them, including mighty Ethiopia, are landlocked, making international trade and economic growth that much more arduous and expensive. Access to navigable rivers is limited, natural harbors are few, soils are poor and thin, several countries largely consist of miles and miles of sand, and tropical diseases have sapped the strength and productivity of innumerable millions. Being landlocked, having few resources (although countries along Africa's west coast have tapped into deep offshore petroleum and gas reservoirs), and being beset by malaria, tuberculosis, schistosomiasis, AIDS, and many other maladies has kept much of Africa poor for centuries.

Thirty-two of the world's poorest 44 countries are African. Hunger is common. So is rapid deforestation and desertification. Unemployment rates are often over 50 percent, for jobs are few—even in agriculture. Where Africa once was a land of small villages and a few large cities, with almost everyone engaged in growing grain or root crops or grazing cattle, camels, sheep, and goats, today more than half of all the more than 1 billion Africans, especially those who live south of the Sahara, reside in towns and cities. Traditional agriculture hardly pays, and a number of countries in Africa—particularly the smaller and more fragile ones—can no longer feed themselves.

There is not one Africa, for the continent is full of contradictions and variety. Of the 750 million people living south of the Sahara, at least 150 million live in Nigeria, 85 million in Ethiopia, 68 million in the Democratic Republic of the Congo, and 49 million in South Africa. By contrast, tiny Djibouti and Equatorial Guinea have fewer than 1 million people each, and prosperous Botswana and Namibia each are under 2.2 million in population. Within some countries, even medium-sized ones like Zambia (12 million), there are a plethora of distinct ethnic groups speaking separate languages. Zambia, typical with its multitude of competing entities, has 70 such peoples, roughly broken down into four language and cultural zones. Three of those languages jostle with English for primacy.

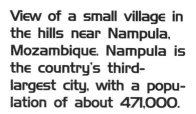

View of a small village in the hills near Nampula, Mozambique. Nampula is the country's third-largest city, with a population of about 471,000.

Indian Ocean fishermen work off the coast of Mozambique. Located in southeastern Africa, Mozambique has approximately 1,550 miles (2,500 km) of coastline—much of it dotted with spectacular beaches.

Given the kaleidoscopic quality of African culture and deep-grained poverty, it is no wonder that Africa has developed economically and politically less rapidly than other regions. Since independence from colonial rule, weak governance has also plagued Africa and contributed significantly to the widespread poverty of its peoples. Only Botswana and offshore Mauritius have been governed democratically without interruption since independence. Both are among Africa's wealthiest countries, too, thanks to the steady application of good governance.

Aside from those two nations, and South Africa, Africa has been a continent of coups since 1960, with massive and oil-rich Nigeria suffering incessant periods of harsh, corrupt, autocratic military rule. Nearly every other country on or around the continent, small and large, has been plagued by similar bouts of instability and dictatorial rule. In the 1970s and 1980s Idi Amin ruled Uganda capriciously and Jean-Bedel Bokassa proclaimed himself emperor of the Central African Republic. Macias Nguema of Equatorial Guinea was another in that same mold. More recently Daniel arap Moi held Kenya in thrall and Robert Mugabe has imposed himself on once-prosperous Zimbabwe. In both of those cases, as in the case of Gnassingbe Eyadema in Togo and the late Mobutu Sese Seko in Congo, these presidents stole wildly and drove entire peoples and their nations into penury. Corruption is common in Africa, and so are a weak rule-of-law framework, misplaced development, high expenditures on soldiers and low expenditures on health and education, and a widespread (but not universal) refusal on the part of leaders to work well for their followers and citizens.

Conflict between groups within countries has also been common in Africa. More than 12 million Africans have been killed in civil wars since 1990, while another 9 million have become refugees. Decades of conflict in Sudan led to a January 2011 referendum in which the people of southern Sudan voted overwhelmingly to secede and form a new state. In early 2011, anti-government protests spread throughout North Africa, ultimately toppling long-standing regimes in Tunisia and Egypt. That same year, there were serious ongoing hostilities within Chad, Ivory Coast, Libya, the Niger Delta region of Nigeria, and Somalia.

Despite such dangers, despotism, and decay, Africa is improving. Botswana and Mauritius, now joined by South Africa, Senegal, Kenya, and Ghana, are beacons of democratic growth and enlightened rule. Uganda and Senegal are taking the lead in combating and reducing the spread of AIDS, and others are following. There are serious signs of the kinds of progressive economic policy changes that might lead to prosperity for more of Africa's peoples. The trajectory in Africa is positive.

The former Portuguese colony of Mozambique is a land of palm tree plantations, mangrove forests, and white sandy beaches. (Opposite) A popular resort can be found at Vilanculos Beach, in Inhambane. (Right) The Limpopo River winds its way through southern Mozambique.

An Undeveloped Gem

LOCATED ON THE SOUTHEASTERN COAST of Africa, the Republic of Mozambique contains coastal lowlands, high *plateaus*, and mountains. The country has many valuable but undeveloped resources, including natural gas, coal, and titanium. Because of a brutal 16-year civil war, which ended in 1992, Mozambique has suffered numerous environmental, economic, and social problems. The country is one of the poorest, most undeveloped nations in the world, although it has made economic progress in recent years.

THE LAND

Mozambique is bordered on the north by Tanzania; on the west by Malawi, Zambia, and Zimbabwe; and on the south by Swaziland and South Africa.

THE GEOGRAPHY OF MOZAMBIQUE

Location: Southeastern Africa, bordering on the Mozambique Channel (an arm of the Indian Ocean), between South Africa and Tanzania

Area: (about twice the size of California)
   total: 308,642 square miles (799,380 sq km)
   land: 303,623 square miles (786,380 sq km)
   water: 5,019 square miles (13,000 sq km)

Borders: Malawi, 975 miles (1,569 km); South Africa, 305 miles (491 km); Swaziland, 65 miles (105 km); Tanzania, 470 miles (756 km); Zambia, 260 miles (419 km), Zimbabwe, 765 miles (1,231 km)

Climate: tropical to subtropical

Terrain: mostly coastal lowlands, uplands in center, high plateaus in northwest, mountains in west

Elevation extremes:
   lowest point: Indian Ocean, 0 feet (0 meters)
   highest point: Monte Binga, 7,992 feet (2,436 meters)

Natural hazards: severe droughts; devastating cyclones and floods in central and southern provinces

Source: CIA World Factbook, 2011

Almost twice the size of California, Mozambique consists of about 308,642 square miles (799,3 square kilometers) of territory. Of that area, 303,623 square miles (786,380 sq km) is land and about 5,019 square miles (13,000 sq km) is water.

The country of Mozambique has one of the longest coastlines of Africa: approximately 1,535 miles (2,470 km) of the land is bordered on the east by the Indian Ocean. The southern shorelines feature beaches of white sand, while at the far northern shores, rocky cliffs guard the coast.

The northern coast is also lined with coral reefs, and many small coral islands dot the waters.

About half of Mozambique's land consists of low-lying plateaus that extend inland from the coast. They are covered by *savannas*—dry, open grasslands dotted by trees. Tracts of hardwood forests can also be found on the plateaus.

In western Mozambique, these low plains give way to mountainous terrain patched with hardwood forests. At the country's western border with Zimbabwe lie two major mountain ranges: the Inyanga and Chimanimani. Monte Binga, the nation's highest point, which reaches 7,992 feet (2,436 meters), is part of the Chimanimani mountain range.

In south-central parts of Mozambique, the rolling plains are interrupted by a series of hills named the Serra Da Gorongosa. These hills are part of Gorongosa National Park, Mozambique's largest national park, which covers more than 2,000 square miles (5,180 sq km) of forests, grasslands, and swamps. Farther south, the Lebombo Mountains separate Mozambique from South Africa.

Twenty-five major rivers flow eastward through the country, before emptying into the Indian Ocean. Among them are the Lúrio, Lugela, Revùe, Save, Limpopo, Incomati, Zambezi, and Rovuma. The Zambezi, with a length of 1,650 miles (2,655 km), is the country's largest river and the fourth-largest river in all of Africa. It cuts through the middle of the country, entering Mozambique at its border with Zambia and Zimbabwe and emptying into the Mozambique Channel. This channel, located between Mozambique and the island nation of Madagascar, is a deep expanse of water that is part of the Indian Ocean.

Several large lakes can be found in Mozambique. To the northwest is Lake Nyasa (also called Lake Malawi), which forms part of Mozambique's boundary with Malawi. It is the third-largest lake in Africa—about 348 miles (560 km) long and 47 miles (75 km) across at its widest point. In western Mozambique lies Lake Cahora Bassa, which was formed by damming the Zambezi River. With a surface area of 1,057 square miles (2,739 sq km), the Cahora Bassa is the second-largest artificially made lake in Africa.

CLIMATE

Because Mozambique has a mainly *tropical* climate, the weather is generally mild and warm enough to support plant growth year round. However, temperatures and rainfall can vary greatly from one region to another. The nation is prone to weather extremes. Severe droughts and devastating storms, especially in recent years, have caused great hardship in the country.

The Republic of Mozambique is located south of the equator, so its seasons fall at opposite times of the year than they do in countries north of the equator. Winter in Mozambique occurs from June to September, and summer runs from December to March. The average temperature in the country is 68° Fahrenheit (20° Celsius) during the winter months, and 80°F (27°C) at the height of the nation's summer, in January.

Although the temperature remains warm year round, Mozambique usually sees less precipitation than other tropical areas. Rainfall averages between 16 to 48 inches (41 to 122 centimeters) per year. Most precipitation falls during the rainy season, which runs from November to March.

VEGETATION

Mozambique's forests cover nearly 25 percent of the land. In general, the loss of tree cover, or deforestation, has not been an issue in Mozambique, as it is in many other African nations. Since 1990, only about 4 percent of the country's forests have been lost.

Among Mozambique's common trees are coconut palms and date palms that thrive along the coast and rivers. Mangroves line the edges of rivers and coastal swamps, where they grow among plants such as spear grass, bamboo, and papyrus. Valuable hardwoods such as East African mahogany, mopani, and ebony can be found in the forests and grasslands.

Hardwoods like East African mahogany, or *khaya nyasica*, and mopani are used to make furniture and in the creation of elaborate woodcarvings by some **indigenous** people of Mozambique, particularly the Makonde. However, Makonde artisans usually work with ebony, known in Swahili as *mpingo*, in their artwork and other wooden crafts.

Ebony is a valuable timber export because it is used in the manufacture of musical instruments, such as oboes, bagpipes, and clarinets. Because the tree is abundant in Mozambique and nearby Tanzania, its harvesting has become a vital part of the nation's economy. However, ebony has been over-harvested in other countries in Africa, particularly Kenya, and there are movements to restrict its export in Mozambique and Tanzania in order to preserve the tree.

The most impressive tree in Mozambique's grasslands is the baobab. Considered by many people as a symbol of Africa, the baobab is a massive

The unique branches of the baobab tree look like roots growing into the air.

tree that can live for as long as a thousand years. Its twisted branches produce hanging fruits up to 1 foot (30 cm) long. Both animals and humans depend on the fruit as a source of food. People also use the leaves of the baobab for medicines and its bark to make baskets, paper, rope, cloth, and many other items.

A common tree in Mozambique is the cashew. Native to South America, cashew nut trees were brought from Brazil to Africa by Portuguese explorers during the 16th and 17th centuries. Today, farmers grow cashew nuts as an export crop, but the trees can also be found growing in the wild.

WILDLIFE AND MARINELIFE

Mozambique contains a diversity of wildlife, with at least 685 species of birds, 228 kinds of reptiles, 195 different types of mammals, and 59 kinds of amphibians. Lake Nyasa is home to a variety of fish, including the chambo, kampango, and tilapia, the latter of which is prized for its flavorful meat. The Mozambique Channel supports sharks, porpoises, manta rays, and warm-water fish. These coastal waters contain a variety of other marinelife, including lobsters, crabs, tuna, swordfish, squid, and many brightly colored fish.

The waters off the coast of Mozambique boast a huge number of the living organisms that form coral. Along the southern coastline, around the islands of the Bazaruto *Archipelago*, are coral reefs that are home to more than 2,000 species of fish, as well as mollusks, turtles, and sharks. In northern Mozambique, the Quirimbas Archipelago has one of the richest areas of coral reef in the world. Surrounding 11 islands, the reefs consist of more than 55 kinds of coral, the highest coral species diversity on the coast of East Africa. These reefs are home to nearly 400 species of fish and a variety of mollusks.

The lakes in northeastern Mozambique provide *habitats* for vast flocks of water birds, including flamingos. The beautiful birds get their pink coloring from the shrimp they eat. Other lake dwellers include crocodiles and hippopotamuses.

The rolling plains and grasslands of Mozambique contain numerous large mammals, including elephants, lions, giraffes, zebras, antelope, impalas, and buffalo. It is not unusual to see hawks, eagles, vultures, and crows flying overhead. Smaller birds, such as partridges and quail, make their homes in tangles of brush along the edges of forested areas.

Mozambique contains many dangerous reptiles. Poisonous vipers, cobras, and puff adders are common. One deadly reptile is the giant African python. It is the largest of all snakes, growing 18 to 20 feet (5.5 to 6 meters) long; some have been known to reach 28 feet (8.5 meters). The python is a constrictor: Instead of killing with venom, it uses its strong body to squeeze its prey to death.

ENVIRONMENTAL CONCERNS

Mozambique's coral reefs have been threatened by overharvesting, global warming, and pollution. People harvest coral to sell for making jewelry, decorating aquariums, and other purposes. Scientists believe that global warming is causing sea temperatures to become abnormally warm, and high water temperatures can kill coral. In 1998, many of the world's coral reefs, including some off the coast of Mozambique, were killed when sea temperatures rose. Reef damage has also been caused in Mozambique by industry pollution and agricultural runoff. In the late 1990s, in an effort to protect its coral reefs, Mozambique banned the sale of coral skeletons and stony corals.

Humans have also had an impact on Mozambique's large mammals. As people have moved into animal habitats, their presence has reduced wildlife populations. Farmers kill hippos and elephants to prevent them from damaging crops. These animals are also killed by *poachers* for their skin, valuable ivory tusks, and meat.

African lions have been adversely affected by their loss of habitat, too. In the early 1990s, about 50,000 lions lived freely in Africa. Today that number has dwindled to around 12,500. Habitat destruction plays a part in the lions' decline. But, some wild cats have also been killed by farmers trying to protect their livestock.

During the 1980s and 1990s poaching reduced the populations of large mammals in Gorongosa National Park by more than 95 percent. Beginning in 2006, a large number of animals have been reintroduced to Gorongosa as part of the Park Restoration Project, including zebras, wildebeest, elephants, hip-

The common hippo lives in lakes and river systems throughout Mozambique. Its numbers were severely reduced during the country's civil war.

pos, and buffalo. In addition to those already mentioned, the park is home to cheetahs, warthogs, and an increasing population of lions. It also has around 500 species of birds, many of which can be found only in the park. They include the green-headed oriole, the moustached warbler, the bluethroated sunbird, and the chestnut-fronted Helmut shrike.

Park rangers train in Gorongosa National Park, which is located in central Mozambique. The rangers learn conservation techniques, as well as how to protect the wild animals in the park from poachers.

In 2002, the governments of Zimbabwe, South Africa, and Mozambique signed a treaty to create one of the largest conservation parks in the world: the Great Limpopo Transfrontier Park. When complete, the 13,500-square-mile (35,000-sq-km) park will link Limpopo National Park in Mozambique; Kruger National Park in South Africa; and Gonarezhou National Park, Manjinji Pan Sanctuary, and Malipati Safari Area in Zimbabwe. The resulting transfrontier park will allow animals to freely cross international borders, expanding their range and allowing migration. It is also hoped that local communities will benefit from *ecotourism* that the immense park will bring to the area.

The transfrontier park moved closer becoming a reality with the opening of the Giriyondo Access Facility between Limpopo and Kruger national parks in August 2006. However, the Great Limpopo Transfrontier Park will not be officially opened until further sections of the fence between the three countries are removed, allowing free movement of animals and people along the length of the international borders within the boundaries of the park. This will take many years to implement.

To reduce poaching and protect wildlife habitats, the government of Mozambique has created protected areas that cover almost 6 percent of the nation. They include national parks such as Gorongosa and Limpopo, as well as Maputo Elephant Reserve, where wildlife can migrate between Mozambique and South Africa. As it finds the funding, the government hopes to add more national park systems and wildlife preserves.

(Opposite) View from a fort on Mozambique Island, the capital of Portugal's East Africa colony. After almost 500 years under Portuguese rule, Mozambique achieved independence in 1975. (Right) An expert teaches Manica Province residents how to avoid landmines left from the country's civil war. The government hopes all mined areas will be cleared by 2014.

2 The Hard Road to Independence

THE EASTERN PORTION of Africa is often called the cradle of civilization because anthropologists and archeologists consider it the birthplace of mankind. Hundreds of thousands of years ago, the first humans appeared in what is now known as Kenya and Ethiopia. From these regions, some of the first people migrated to today's Mozambique.

EARLY PEOPLES

Based on their work with fossils, cave drawings, and primitive tools discovered in the region, scientists believe that the first people to live in Mozambique arrived around 4000 B.C. Ancestors of the *ethnic group* known today as the Khoisan, these early people were nomads, moving from place to place in search of the resources that they needed to survive.

23

They lived in caves, hunted animals, and gathered wild fruits, nuts, and roots for food.

Some time before 1300 B.C. these people began banding into more organized tribes. They developed hunting tools, fashioning baskets to catch fish, and using snares and other traps to capture prey. Bows and arrows, sometimes laced with poisons, were used to kill larger game.

Around the first century A.D. Bantu-speaking people from north-central Africa arrived. The Bantu tribes traveled through the Zambezi River Valley and eventually spread into the plateau and coastal regions, displacing the hunter-gatherers. The new arrivals were taller and darker-skinned than the native people. More scientifically advanced, the Bantu used iron-making technology to make the weapons needed to conquer their neighbors and the tools needed to farm the land.

EAST AFRICAN TRADE

Around A.D. 800 Arab traders made contact with the people living in African coastal seaports and cities. The Arabs soon established a profitable trade with the Bantu, offering ceramics, cloth, beads, salt, and metal goods in exchange for African items such as gold, palm oil, amber, and ivory. Over the centuries, the Arabs made alliances with the people living along the coast and intermarried with them. The African and Arabian languages and customs eventually blended into a new language and culture called Swahili.

Between the 12th and 18th centuries, the Swahili trading centers grew, many becoming *city-states* that flourished from trade with Arabia, India, and China. Trade routes also connected the coastal cities with gold mines and agricultural centers located in the interior of Africa. Some of the major city-states included Sofala, on the northeastern coast of today's Mozambique; Cuama, along the Zambezi River; and Inhambane, on the southeastern coast.

The Arabs brought their religious faith of Islam, which was adopted by many Africans. People who practice Islam, called Muslims, follow the teachings of the Prophet Muhammad (ca. 570–632 A.D.), who taught his followers to submit themselves to the will of God, or Allah, in all aspects of life.

PORTUGUESE CONTROL

In the late 1400s the king of Portugal, Manuel I, called on explorer Vasco da Gama to find a shipping route that would enable Portugal to establish trade with India. The king wanted his country to take part in the profitable spice trade, and he also wanted access to the gold being mined in Africa.

Commanding four ships and a crew of about 170 men, da Gama sailed from Lisbon, Portugal, on July 8, 1497. He headed south

This watercolor painting depicts Portuguese explorer Vasco da Gama, who landed on the coast of Mozambique during his historic voyage to India (1497–99). Within a decade, Portugal had conquered many coastal cities in the region and made them outposts for the Portuguese Indian Ocean trade network.

toward Africa's southern tip, the Cape of Good Hope. After rounding the Cape, da Gama and his men turned north. In 1498, they stopped at several African trade centers along the eastern coast of Africa, including Inhambane and Moçambique.

The Swahilis and Arab traders in Moçambique did not welcome the explorers. Aware that the Portuguese threatened their control of trade in the region, the Swahilis tried to seize the Portuguese ships. But da Gama and his men escaped and continued on their journey to India.

Other Portuguese explorers followed. Among them were Pedro Alvares Cabral and Sancho de Tovar, who traveled to Sofala and Moçambique between 1500 and 1502. These cities fell to the Portuguese just a few years later. In 1505 nobleman and explorer Francisco de Almeida took over Moçambique, while Pedro de Anhaia assumed control of nearby Sofala. Within a few years, the Portuguese were in charge of many of the trading posts along Africa's east coast.

The interior of Africa was next. One Portuguese trader who made his way inland was Antonio Fernandes. In the early 1500s, he visited the Mwanamutapa Kingdom, which controlled the area between the Save and Zambezi Rivers. Founded in the 1400s by the Shona people, it had established great wealth through the gold trade. Much of the gold mined in the area passed through Mwanamutapa on its way to be exported by Swahili traders in Sofala.

In an effort to obtain control of the gold trade, the Portuguese occupied the region around the lower Zambezi River. In 1531 Portuguese forces established military and trading posts (today's cities of Tete and Sena) on the river. Later attempts to conquer Mwanamutapa failed, but by the end of the 1500s,

To enforce order among the Africans, the Portuguese rulers used gunboats like this one, which is tied up on the Zambezi River.

the Portuguese had established a trading center on the island of Mozambique and taken control of trade south of the island.

COLONIAL RULE

During the early 1600s, Portugal began to *colonize* the area. In 1629, the government began granting land to Portuguese settlers. They established large farming estates, called *prazos*. Native Africans were forced to work on the *prazos* as slaves or as members of private armies for the owners. By the 18th and 19th centuries, many *prazo* owners were involved with the slave trade. Some African tribal chiefs also took part in the sale of Africans, by selling captives caught in tribal battles into slavery.

Portuguese attempts to take control of more of the region continued. Many African tribes, including the Shangaan, the Barue, the Yao, and the Makua, resisted European rule. Although the Portuguese had larger numbers in their armies, the would-be conquerors often suffered humiliating defeats.

Mozambican children pose in front of a thatched-roof house in the Portuguese East Africa colony, circa 1923.

Another, more patient, way of conquering the African tribes proved more effective. As Portuguese traders worked their way farther inland, the tribal chiefs in these regions came to rely more heavily on their commerce.

The trading relationship between the Africans and Portuguese eventually accomplished what warfare could not. By the late 1800s the Portuguese had gained control of the entire region that is now Mozambique. Portugal made its claims to the land official in 1885, when the heads of several European nations met in Berlin, Germany. During the Berlin Conference, they agreed to divide up the African continent among themselves. Portugal claimed Mozambique, which it also referred to as Portuguese East Africa. The border established for the country in 1891 is relatively close to the boundaries Mozambique recognizes today.

The job of administering Portuguese East Africa fell to various European charter companies, which were granted *concessions* by the Portuguese government to administer different regions. Three major charter companies in

Mozambique were the Zambezia Company, the Mozambique Company, and the Niassa Company. These organizations continued the *prazo* policies of forced labor. The companies established military posts to protect their holdings and levied taxes on the Mozambicans. Some native Africans were forced to work in mines or on plantations in South Africa and nearby British colonies.

By establishing railroad lines that connected Mozambique with other African nations, the charter companies enabled the colony to develop economically. However, the goals of the charter companies were to make profits for their shareholders and to improve life for the growing numbers of white Portuguese settlers—not for the indigenous people.

In 1933, the Portuguese government passed the Colonial Act, which made Mozambique part of the Portuguese state. The Act established a common law and centrally planned economy for the country. But it also further repressed the indigenous people, forbidding them from working as traders or running their own businesses, and effectively eliminating health and educational opportunities. Those who protested were frequently punished by being exiled, imprisoned, or put to death.

STRUGGLE FOR INDEPENDENCE

By the mid-1900s, native Mozambicans had begun to strongly protest the racial discrimination and forced labor policies of the colonial government. In 1960 farmers from the Makonde ethnic group organized a peaceful demonstration in their northern village of Muedo, to protest being forced by the government to grow cotton. During the demonstration, Portuguese troops shot and killed at least 500 of the protesters. Those who survived the Muedo massacre fled to Tanzania. There they joined other Mozambicans who had left the country earlier because of their opposition to Portuguese rule.

The group was led by Eduardo Mondlane, of the Tsonga tribe. He had been educated in the United States, where he earned a degree in anthropology and sociology at Oberlin College, in Ohio. Mondlane then went on to obtain a master of arts in sociology from Northwestern University, in Chicago, Illinois, and a doctor of philosophy in anthropology from Harvard, in Cambridge, Massachusetts.

After Mondlane returned to Mozambique, he worked to free the country from Portuguese rule. In 1961, he formed a guerrilla movement called Front for the Liberation of Mozambique, or Frelimo. Three years later, it began carrying out a series of attacks against the Mozambique government. In time, the rebels gained control over the northern portion of the country.

Meanwhile, the Portuguese tried to win support from Mozambicans and the international community by working to improve the country's economy. One colonial economic development project was the Cahora Bassa, a huge hydroelectric project aimed at providing electricity for the people of Mozambique as well as for export to other countries.

However, Portugal's efforts came too late. Tired of centuries of oppression, the Mozambicans increasingly supported Frelimo. Even the assassination of its leader, Mondlane, in 1969, didn't stop the rebels. Samora Machel, one of Mondlane's followers, stepped in to head the movement.

By 1971, the rebellion had spread to the Tete Province, in central Mozambique. In efforts to turn Mozambicans against one another and end the uprising, the Portuguese tried to stir up old tribal rivalries. The colonial government recruited armies of natives to fight Frelimo and punished those who would not join. In at least one case, the Portuguese had hundreds of people burned to death because their community had offered aid to Frelimo. Yet the rebels continued to fight.

During the 1970s, the Portuguese government was also dealing with problems at home. In 1974, army officers who had become dissatisfied with the administration successfully overthrew the Portuguese government. The administration established after the military coup wanted to end the fighting in Africa.

In September 1974, the new Portuguese government agreed to a peace treaty with Frelimo—called the

Frelimo representative Sharfuddine M. Khan (front) asks the United Nations to intervene in the Mozambique conflict, 1971.

Lusaka Agreement—and approved the *decolonization* of Mozambique. The following year, on June 25, 1975, Mozambique became an independent country. Samora Machel, the head of Frelimo, became the nation's first president.

Most of the 250,000 Portuguese living in Mozambique left the country.

SOCIALISM

Frelimo was a *socialist* organization, and Machel quickly moved to have Mozambique's new government follow socialist policies. He nationalized (put under control of the state) privately owned businesses and industries. While the Frelimo government introduced improvements in education and health care, it also restricted political and religious freedoms. No political parties other than Frelimo were legal, and religious schools were closed. Machel developed economic and diplomatic relationships with nations that had similar socialist governments, such as the Soviet Union.

The new country of Mozambique joined several international organizations, such as the United Nations, the *International Monetary Fund* (IMF), and the Organization of African States. In 1976, the United States recognized the Mozambique government, and sent an ambassador and $10 million in financial aid. However, the friendly relationship between the United States and Mozambique did not last. The U.S. government could not support the way socialism was being practiced in the new nation, especially the Frelimo

Samora Machel (1933–1986) became head of the pro-independence party Frelimo after the assassination of Eduardo Mondlane in 1969. When Mozambique became independent in 1975, Machel became the country's first president.

government's refusal to allow opposition parties. The United States accused the Mozambican military and police of violating people's human rights, and threatened to discontinue aid unless conditions improved.

Meanwhile, the government of Mozambique was supporting rebels in other African nations that were still under white-minority rule. When the United Nations placed sanctions against the oppressive white-minority government of Rhodesia in 1976, Mozambique honored the *sanctions*, although it lost significant income.

In South Africa, which was also ruled by a white-minority government, Mozambique aided that country's black majority by supporting its rebel fighters. But this support had a price. While Mozambique helped guerrillas in South Africa, the governments of South Africa and Rhodesia were aiding the Mozambican National Resistance (Renamo), a rebel group fighting against Frelimo. From its base in the central part of the country, Renamo began a civil war against the Mozambique government in the late 1970s. The conflict killed thousands of people and disrupted the nation's agricultural production, which had already been devastated by severe droughts.

In 1984, an agreement to end the fighting between Mozambique and South Africa was reached. But Renamo rebels refused to surrender. Ultimately, Mozambique's civil war lasted for 16 years, causing extreme hardship in an already poor nation. Millions of people died from starvation caused by massive food shortages. Many others fled to other countries.

In an effort to ease the suffering of its citizens, Mozambique's socialist government implemented some political and economic reforms during the

In 1984, Mozambique and other African countries were devastated by drought and famine. Here, grain supplied by the World Food Programme is unloaded at the shallow harbour of Vilanculos, where it will be distributed to the four provinces of southern Mozambique that were most affected by the drought.

1980s. Private ownership was encouraged, and people were allowed to start their own businesses. The government also lessened its control over agricultural production, by allowing individuals to farm their own land.

Machel recognized that other major reforms were necessary, but he never had the chance to enact them. In 1986, he and several of his advisors died in a suspicious plane crash. Some people believe that South Africans opposed to Frelimo might have been involved with the plane crash, although this was not proven.

A NEW DIRECTION

Machel's foreign minister, Joaquim Chissano, became the country's next president. Following Machel's lead, he formally abandoned attempts to make Mozambique a socialist nation, in 1989. The following year, the Mozambique government approved a new constitution that established the country as a republic and granted citizens more freedoms, including freedom of the press and the right to vote in open elections.

In October 1992, Frelimo and Renamo signed a peace treaty that officially ended the civil war. Among other things, it recognized the right of other political parties besides Frelimo to legally exist. Two years later, in 1994, the country held its first presidential election in which more than one party submitted candidates. Chissano was reelected.

Mozambique's future appeared bright. By the end of 1995, most of the 1.7 million people who had fled to other nations during the civil war had returned. Another 4 million citizens who had been internally displaced by

The administration of President Joaquim Alberto Chissano rejected socialism, reforming the government to allow Mozambique's people greater freedom. The political changes helped Mozambique emerge from its civil war.

This aerial photo, taken in March 2000, shows the flooded Save River near the village of Machanga. To help cope with this natural disaster, Mozambique received help from the United States and other countries.

the fighting returned to their homes. In the late 1990s, the nation showed significant economic growth. Confident of the effectiveness of Mozambique's government, numerous countries offered aid to promote further economic development.

But then disaster struck. In February 2000, Cyclone Eline battered Mozambique with heavy rains. Floods devastated the southern part of the country, destroying crops, businesses, and homes. Around 700 people died.

Another 500,000 were left homeless. The following year, the country suffered from more severe flooding. A hundred people died, and more than 200,000 were left homeless.

In response to these disasters, financial and food aid poured in from many other nations. The U.S. Congress granted $137 million in emergency funding to help the weather-ravaged areas. The money was used to help rebuild damaged roads, bridges, railways, and other important *infrastructure*. Foreign aid provided loans to farmers and businesses, while emergency recovery grants helped 106,000 displaced families. However, the damage caused by the storms and flooding was significant, and recovery was slow.

Despite its problems, the country remained politically stable. In compliance with the nation's constitution, Chissano did not seek a third term as president. However, in the December 2004 elections, the Frelimo Party continued to receive strong support from the people of Mozambique. Voters went to the polls and gave Frelimo's candidate, Armando Guebuza—a former leader in Mozambique's independence movement—nearly 64 percent of the vote.

Guebuza was re-elected in October of 2009 by an even larger majority and chose to retain almost all of his first-term ministers. Despite allegations of electoral fraud, there is hope that this continuity will provide the president and his administration an opportunity to address the country's most pressing issues.

A democratic state since 1990, Mozambique held its fourth national elections in 2009. (Opposite) Voters wait in line to vote at a polling station in Xipamanine, a suburb of Maputo. (Right) Armando Emílio Guebuza has served as president of Mozambique since 2005; he was re-elected in 2009 with about 75 percent of the vote.

3 A New Democracy

AFTER HUNDREDS OF YEARS as a Portuguese colony and about 15 years as a socialist country, Mozambique today is a republic. This form of government is one that allows people to elect representatives who govern the state. All citizens at least 18 years of age are eligible to vote.

The nation's constitution, adopted on November 30, 1990, specifies how the Republic of Mozambique is to be governed. The constitution established Portuguese as the official language and divided the country into separate administrative regions. Mozambique is made up of 10 provinces: Cabo Delgado, Gaza, Inhambane, Manica, Maputo, Nampula, Niassa, Sofala, Tete, and Zambezia. The federal government is based in the capital city of Maputo, which has the same status as that of the provinces. They are further divided into 224 districts and 33 municipalities, of which the city of Maputo is the largest.

In addition to defining requirements for citizenship, elections, and other aspects of a republic, the Mozambique constitution describes how the government should run. It consists of three branches: executive, legislative, and judicial.

THE EXECUTIVE BRANCH

The executive branch is headed by the president, or head of state. To become president, a candidate must secure more than half the number of votes cast in the election. If no candidate receives a majority of votes, a second round of voting occurs. At that time, the only names on the ballot are the two candidates who received the most votes in the first round. The president is elected to a five-year term, and may be re-elected for a second five-year term.

In 2005, Luisa Dias Diogo became the first woman to serve as Mozambique's prime minister. She held the post until January 2010.

The president of Mozambique has many responsibilities. They include: serving as commander-in-chief of the country's military, calling general elections, and communicating with the citizens and legislature about issues important to the country. The president may also grant pardons and reduce sentences of people convicted of crimes.

As the head of the executive branch, the president is responsible for choosing high-level government officials such as the prime minister and members of the cabinet, or Council of Ministers. After Armando Guebuza became president in February 2005, he selected Luisa Diogo to serve as prime minister. She was the first woman in Mozambique to hold this powerful position.

The prime minister presides over meetings of the Council of Ministers. He or she also helps the president draw up government programs and plans of action, and then presents them to the legislature for approval. Another role of the prime minister is advising the president on the creation of new ministries and on appointments within various government agencies.

The Council of Ministers consists of 25 members, each of whom is responsible for a different aspect of life in Mozambique. For example, the minister of agriculture keeps tabs on everything related to farming in the

Aires Bonifacio Baptista Ali, the current prime minister of Mozambique, meets with United Nations Secretary-General Ban Ki-moon. Ali previously served as governor of Mozambique's Inhambane Province (2000–2004) and as Minister of Education (2005–2010).

country. The minister of national defense helps the prime minister ensure that the country is protected from any internal or foreign threats. Other cabinet positions in the Mozambique government are the minister of development and planning, the minister of education and culture, the minister of women and social action, and the minister of tourism.

THE LEGISLATIVE BRANCH

The federal legislative body of the Mozambique government is called the Assembly of the Republic. This one-house, or *unicameral*, legislature creates the country's laws. The Assembly of the Republic consists of 250 members, or deputies, who are elected by the country's citizens. Members of the Assembly are elected to five-year terms.

The percentage of votes that groups of candidates receive during elections determines the percentage of seats that parties control in the Assembly. The two largest parties in the nation—Frelimo and Renamo—dominate the legislature, though numerous smaller parties often submit candidates. During the October 2009 elections, Frelimo (with 75 percent of the vote) garnered 191 seats, Renamo (with 18 percent) earned 51, and MDM (with 4 percent) earned the remaining 8.

THE JUDICIAL BRANCH

The judicial branch of a government refers to the system of courts in which justice is administered or disputes resolved. In Mozambique, there are various levels of courts, including district, municipal, provincial, and federal courts.

Members of the Supreme Court, which is Mozambique's federal judicial body, are either appointed by the president or elected by the Assembly of the Republic. As the highest court of the judiciary, the Supreme Court is where final appeals to case decisions are made. Because no separate Constitutional Court has been established, the Supreme Court also reviews cases challenging the constitutionality of laws.

CORRUPTION

Since the 1990s, Mozambique's government, particularly the judicial branch, has developed a reputation for being corrupt and unfair. Judges have been known to take bribes in exchange for releasing suspects. Incriminating evidence has been "lost" and key witnesses frightened into not testifying. Critics have accused government police of using excessive force, and causing death and injury during arrests and imprisonment. Within the executive branch, officials of ministries and regulatory agencies have been known to accept bribes to influence their enforcement of specific laws or regulations.

President Guebuza's government has taken some steps to discipline corrupt judges, police, and ministry officials and to make the country's bureaucracy more responsive to the needs of its citizens. In one highly publicized example from 2010, a former government minister was sentenced to a 20-year prison term for embezzlement. However, reform has been slow, and outsiders agree that access to justice for ordinary people remains difficult.

(Opposite) The giant Cahora Bassa Dam uses the water of the Zambezi River to generate electricity. (Right) Mozambican fishermen and women pull a fishing net from the water. The fishing industry is an important segment of Mozambique's economy.

4 A Struggling Economy

MOZAMBIQUE IS ONE of the world's poorest nations. Its 16-year civil war destroyed much of its infrastructure and took thousands of lives. About half of the population depends on food aid to survive. Approximately 70 percent of Mozambique's citizens live below the poverty line. Twenty-one percent of working-age people are unemployed.

AGRICULTURE AND FISHING

While around 80 percent of Mozambique's workers are farmers, only about 20 percent of Mozambique's annual *gross domestic product* (GDP) comes from the agricultural sector. GDP refers to the total value of all the goods and services produced in a country within a given year. Although approximately four out of five people in the nation's workforce are farmers, most

THE ECONOMY OF MOZAMBIQUE

Gross domestic product (GDP*):
$21.81 billion
Inflation: 13.5%
Natural resources: coal, titanium, natural gas, hydropower, tantalum, graphite
Agriculture (28.8% of GDP): cotton, cashew nuts, sugarcane, tea, cassava (tapioca), corn, coconuts, sisal, citrus and tropical fruits, potatoes, sunflowers, beef, poultry
Industry (26% of GDP): food, beverages, chemicals (fertilizer, soap, paints), aluminum, petroleum products, textiles, cement, glass, asbestos, tobacco
Services (45.2% of GDP): government, tourism

Foreign trade:
Exports—$2.517 billion: aluminum, prawns, cashews, cotton, sugar, citrus, timber, bulk electricity
Imports—$3.527 billion: machinery and equipment, vehicles, fuel, chemicals, metal products, foodstuffs, textiles
Economic growth rate: 7%
Currency exchange rate: U.S. $1 = 28.75 meticals (2011)

*GDP is the total value of goods and services produced in a country annually.
All figures are 2010 estimates unless otherwise indicated.
Source: CIA World Factbook, 2011.

of them practice subsistence agriculture—that is, they raise only enough food to feed their own families. As a result, agricultural production does not contribute toward increasing the nation's wealth.

Farmers in Mozambique raise animals such as goats, cattle, and poultry and grow crops such as tea, cotton, sunflowers, sugar cane, corn, potatoes, fruit, coconuts, and *cassava*. Cashew nuts, which are produced mostly in the provinces of Cabo Delgado, Nampula, and Zambezia, are among the country's top exports.

Mozambique's 1,550-mile (2,500-km) coastline and marine resources provide for a strong fishing industry. For many years, prawns and other seafood have been major exports.

INDUSTRY

Although only 6 percent of the labor force works in industry, this sector accounts for about 30 percent of gross domestic product. Factories in Mozambique process foods, refine oil, and manufacture textiles, glass, construction materials, asbestos, tobacco, fertilizers, soap, and paints. Mining operations extract coal, salt, and bauxite, and hydroelectric plants on Mozambique's great rivers generate electricity.

One of the most important hydroelectric plants is the Cahora Bassa Dam, built by the Portuguese on the Zambezi

A Mozambican woman tends a vegetable garden in the Maputo green belt.

River near Tete. Completed in 1976, the dam produces a significant amount of electric power, much of which is exported to South Africa. In December 2006, the Portuguese officially transferred majority ownership of the facility to the Mozambique government.

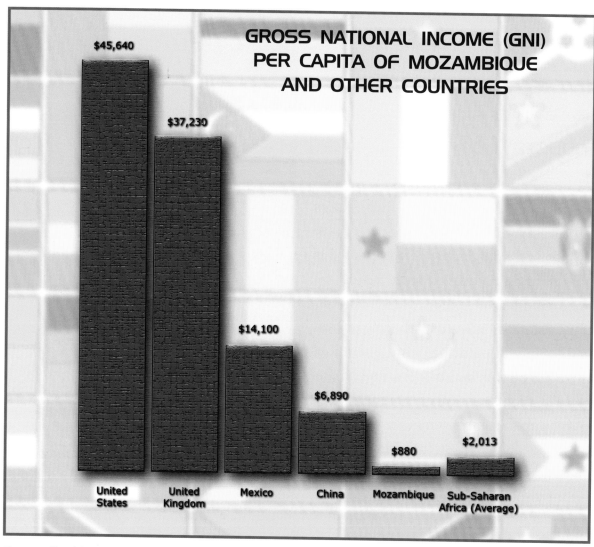

GROSS NATIONAL INCOME (GNI) PER CAPITA OF MOZAMBIQUE AND OTHER COUNTRIES

$45,640 — United States
$37,230 — United Kingdom
$14,100 — Mexico
$6,890 — China
$880 — Mozambique
$2,013 — Sub-Saharan Africa (Average)

Gross national income per capita is the total value of all goods and services produced domestically in a year, supplemented by income received from abroad, divided by midyear population. The above figures take into account fluctuations in currency exchange rates and differences in inflation rates across global economies, so that an international dollar has the same purchasing power as a U.S. dollar has in the United States. Source: World Bank, 2011.

Until the 1970s, Mozambique was the world's leading producer of cashew nuts, which were grown and processed (shelled) in factories in the country. However, by the early 2000s, Mozambique's prosperous cashew nut industry had collapsed, as a result of civil conflict and changes in trade policies. Processing factories closed down, and approximately 10,000 factory workers lost their jobs. Today, most cashew nuts are exported unshelled to India, where they are processed.

SERVICES AND TRANSPORTATION

About 13 percent of Mozambique workers are employed in the service sector, which includes jobs in shops, within the government, and in tourism. This sector has been increasing in recent years and now makes up almost half of Mozambique's economy. Tourism had been an important part of the country's economy before years of civil unrest caused it to sharply decline. Recent efforts have reversed that decline as a now peaceful Mozambique looks to attract vacationers to its tropical beaches and ecotourists to its national parks and preserves.

The transportation industry makes up an important part of the country's service economy. Landlocked nations such as Malawi, Zimbabwe, and Zambia pay Mozambique to use its seaports and railroads to import and export goods. The country's railroad system includes more than 1,926 miles (3,100 km) of track.

Despite showing some economic improvement, Mozambique continues to be a relatively undeveloped nation. Although it has more than 18,640 miles (30,000 km) of roadways, the great majority of these roads remain unpaved. Industrial development is limited, as well, although new industrial opportunities are being created with the help of foreign aid and investment.

FOREIGN INVESTMENT

One of the most significant foreign investment projects is the Mozambique Aluminum (MOZAL) *smelter*, built on the outskirts of Maputo. The nation's largest foreign investment project, the $1.3 billion aluminum smelter began production in the mid-2000s. An international consortium composed of London-based Billiton owns 47 percent of the business; Mitsubishi of Japan owns 25 percent; South Africa's Industrial Development Corporation owns

Foreign investors have financed the construction of resorts and hotels, such as this one near Maputo, and helped to develop Mozambique's tourist industry. In 2011, the World Bank announced a $3 million investment to create jobs and boost sustainable conservation by building a new ecotourist resort in the Maputo Elephant Reserve.

Beira International Airport, on the central coast of Mozambique, is one of the country's three major airports.

24 percent; and the government of Mozambique claims the remaining 4 percent. About 7,000 temporary jobs were created during the facility's construction, and the now operational smelter employs about 800 full-time staff. Along with two other smelters built in southern Africa, MOZAL produces around 5 percent of the world's aluminum. This sector generates earnings of around $1.3 billion per year.

Foreign investment has made possible the extraction of natural gas from onshore fields in Inhambane Province. The South African petrochemical company Sasol finances the extraction of this valuable resource and its transport by pipeline to South Africa.

South Africans who have developed a strong tourist industry within their own country have recently been heavily investing in hotel, ecotourism, and other projects in Mozambique. Foreign investment in sugar and tobacco farms has also helped improve the yield of these agricultural exports.

FOREIGN DEBT AND TRADE

Civil war, high-interest loans, and government mismanagement pushed Mozambique into debt. By 1998, the country's foreign debt stood at around $5.7 billion. Relief came through an IMF and World Bank program developed to help very poor nations deal with unmanageable debt burdens—the Heavily Indebted Poor Countries (HIPC) initiative. Mozambique was the first African nation to receive debt relief through the HIPC initiative: some loans were forgiven and payments for others rescheduled. The country's debt was reduced further in December 2005, when the IMF formally cancelled all of Mozambique's IMF debt contracted before January 1, 2005.

In 2006, aluminum ingots, natural gas, and electricity accounted for 70 percent of the country's exports. Most of the other 30

The currency of Mozambique is called the metical.

per cent of export earnings came from tobacco, prawns, sugar, cotton, and cashew nuts. Mozambique's biggest trading partners include South Africa, the Netherlands, Portugal, Malawi, Australia, Spain, and the United States.

ECONOMIC IMPROVEMENT

A gross domestic product growth rate of more than 7 percent in 2005 has continued a trend of high economic growth that began in 1994. Many economists believe the rebounding growth is due to the political stability of the country, as well as reforms made by the government that include tighter control of spending and the money supply. Economic improvements are also thought to be the result of the government moving away from state ownership of businesses to private ownership. Since Mozambique has moved from socialism to democracy, more than 1,200 government-owned businesses have been put back into private hands.

Mozambique continues to receive massive financial support from donor countries. Almost half of the country's state budget is funded by foreign donors, which include the World Bank, the African Development Bank, the United States, and the European Union.

The nearly 23 million residents of Mozambique tend to maintain traditional African practices. (Opposite) Two women converse outside the central market in Maputo. (Right) In many rural villages, Mozambicans typically live in mud and straw huts.

5 A Traditional Way of Life

DESPITE CENTURIES OF INFLUENCE from Arab traders and Portuguese colonizers, the people of Mozambique have held on to their traditional culture. They display their traditions in many ways—in the colorful African fabrics that they wear, in their art and music, and in the languages they speak.

MAJOR ETHNIC GROUPS

The majority of the people of Mozambique live along the coast and in the fertile valleys of the country's many rivers. Almost all of them are members of indigenous tribal groups.

Living mostly in the north are the 4 million Makhuwa, who make up the country's largest ethnic group. Members of the Makonde, Yao, and Lomwe tribes are also found mostly in northern Mozambique.

THE PEOPLE OF MOZAMBIQUE

Population: 22,948,858 (July 2011 est.)

Ethnic groups: African 99.66% (Makhuwa, Tsonga, Lomwe, Sena, and others), Europeans 0.06%, Euro-Africans 0.2%, Indians 0.08%

Age structure:
  0–14 years: 45.9%
  15–64 years: 51.1%
  65 years and over: 3%

Birth rate: 39.62 births/1,000 population

Infant mortality rate: 78.95 deaths/1,000 live births

Death rate: 13 deaths/1,000 population

Population growth rate: 2.44%

Life expectancy at birth:
  total population: 51.78 years
  male: 51.01 years
  female: 52.57 years

Total fertility rate: 5.46 children born/woman

Religions: Catholic 28.4%, Muslim 17.9%, Zionist Christian 15.5%, Evangelical Pentacostal 10.9%, Anglican 1.3%, other 7.2%, none 18.7% (2007 census)

Languages: Emakhuwa 25.3%, Portuguese (official) 10.7%, Xichangana 10.3%, Cisena 7.5%, Elomwe 7%, Echuwabo 5.1%, other Mozambican languages 30.1%, other 4% (2007 census)

Literacy: 47.8% (2003 est.)

All figures are 2011 estimates unless otherwise indicated.
Source: Adapted from CIA World Factbook, 2011.

In central Mozambique, the Sena and Ndau peoples dominate the Zambezi valley, although many Tsonga (Mozambique's second-largest ethnic group, which includes the Thonga, Tonga, and Shangaan) and Chewa also call this area home. Most of the Tsonga people live in the south, while the Shona people farm the land in the west. The Swahilis reside mostly along the country's coast.

Less than 1 percent of the population of Mozambique consists of foreigners. Most of them are people of Arab, European, or Indian descent.

LANGUAGE

Although Portuguese is the nation's official language, fewer than 11 percent of Mozambicans can speak or read it. Those who are fluent in Portuguese live in the country's major cities. Some citizens use English to conduct business activities, but most people speak one of the many Bantu languages. The most common are Emakhuwa, Xichangana, Elomwe, Cisena, and Echuwabo.

ART AND MUSIC

In far northern Mozambique, Makonde artisans are recognized for their skill in creating intricate carvings out of ebony, a strong black hardwood. Their carvings follow traditions dating back hundreds of years. Traditionally the Makonde carvers would create a stylized figure of a woman, which would be carried for protection from harm. Artisans also create ebony masks used during dance ceremonies, statues, and a special wind instrument known as the *lupembe*.

African traditions are passed on in the stories, poetry, music, and dance of Mozambique. In an effort to preserve and share art forms of the Mozambican people, the government has funded cultural organizations that perform traditional dances, often accompanied by storytelling and choral or instrumental music. The National Song and Dance Company of Mozambique works to promote the country's national culture by performing traditional dances and stories at events in the country and abroad.

A more recent popular form of Mozambican music is *marrabenta*. Originating in Maputo, *marrabenta* combines Portuguese influence with tra-

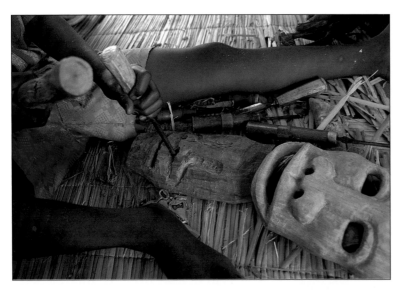

A Makonde sculptor uses chisels to carve wooden masks. In the traditional societies of Mozambique, such masks were used during special ceremonies, such as the coming-of-age ritual performed by young men.

ditional rhythms to create lively urban dance music.

Several Mozambican artists are known throughout the world. Victor Sousa expresses himself in engravings, drawings, paintings, and ceramics. Elias Abdula Naguib uses the canvas to share the story of Mozambique's civil war and reconstruction. Some of Naguib's works are part of the permanent collection displayed at the National Museum in Maputo. One of the most well-regarded Mozambican artists is Malangatana, who works in various mediums, including drawing, ceramics, sculpture, poetry, and music. He is particularly known for his murals and other paintings that portray historical and political events of the colonial era and civil war in Mozambique.

EDUCATION

When Mozambique was a Portuguese colony, few blacks received an education. As a result, in 1975, when the country gained independence, approximately 93 percent of Mozambicans could not read or write. Most of today's political leaders were not educated in government-run public institutions. Instead, they typically learned how to read and write in schools operated by missionaries.

While the educational system has improved since the country became independent, few people ages 25 and older have gone to school for more than two years. As a result, most Mozambicans still cannot read or write. The numbers for women are especially alarming. While 63.5 percent of men who are 15 years old or older can read and write, only 32.7 percent of women in this age group have learned these skills.

The government is working to increase literacy for all citizens. In 2006 officials reported that more than 500 new schools that would serve more than 300,000 pupils had been built and that more than 9,000 teachers had been recruited. The government also eliminated fees required for primary education, which in the past had prevented many lower-income families from sending their children to school.

Although more children are attending school, the educational system in Mozambique is deficient because of a lack of qualified teachers and adequate facilities.

A 2007 report by the United Kingdom's Department for International Development found that the number of primary school students in Mozambique's schools had nearly tripled over a ten-year period, from 1.3 million in 1995 to 3.8 million in 2005. However, the report also noted that a million children still do not go to school, most from poor rural families, and that almost half of all teachers in Mozambique are unqualified.

Because of poverty and high illiteracy rates most people do not get their news and information from newspapers or magazines. Instead, they depend on government-run radio stations for communication. In urban areas, privately run radio stations broadcast across the airwaves, but private stations don't reach into the rural parts of the country.

LOCAL CUISINE

In Mozambique, mealtime is family time. In most households, everyone gathers around the table, where meals are relatively informal. They serve as a time for family members to relax and enjoy one another's company.

The Portuguese influence is evident in the cuisine of Mozambique. It can be seen in the foods that Mozambican farmers grow (cashews, cassava, and tropical fruits) and in the dishes their families create.

Dinner might start with a clam and peanut stew containing crushed red peppers to give the dish a spicy kick. Black olives, green salads, and Portuguese wines and cheeses are a typical part of the meal. But no Mozambican table is complete without *piri-piri*, a hot pepper sauce that adds some fire to any dish.

In areas along the coast, where fishing is a way of life, seafood is a main ingredient in every diet. Local dishes may include crabmeat, giant prawns, squid, grilled shellfish, and dried fish.

In rural Mozambique, people rely mainly on dishes created from the root of the cassava plant. The root can be used in many ways. It can be baked, dried in the sun, ground into meal, or even mashed with water to form a type of porridge. Cassava may also be ground with corn into flour that can be mixed with cassava leaves and water to create a thick dough that is served with roasted nuts.

POVERTY AND DISEASE

The majority of people in Mozambique are very poor. They struggle every day to feed themselves and their families, and many go to bed hungry every night. Because of poor nutrition and the prevalence of diseases such as typhoid fever, hepatitis, and malaria, the life expectancy for the average citizen of Mozambique is less than 40 years.

Many lives have been cut short by acquired immune deficiency syndrome (AIDS). In 2011, 1.4 million Mozambicans (11.5 percent of the adult population) were living with the human immunodeficiency virus (HIV) that causes AIDS or living with the disease itself.

To help stop the spread of AIDS, the Mozambique government and international organizations such as the United Nations are working to educate people in the country about the disease. Many people are ignorant about how AIDS is transmitted or unaware that they are infected. They are being helped by government-supported educational programs that provide counseling services and lessons on reproductive health.

Poor Mozambicans sift through garbage in a landfill near Maputo, looking for food or useful items. Most people in Mozambique are very poor.

A small group of street children in Maputo inform pedestrians about the risks of unsafe sex and demonstrate the proper use of condoms to prevent HIV infection. This activity is organized by the Baixa Centre, created by Médecins du Monde.

Overall health care in Mozambique is poor. When the country gained its independence, Portuguese doctors and nurses fled the country. Although Frelimo set up an emergency program to train paramedics skilled in emergency first aid and routine health care, the government alone could not replace the large number of skilled professionals. However, many religious missions established during Mozambique's colonial period continued to operate, and they offered medical care as well. Today, the Eduardo Mondlane University in Maputo trains many doctors, but much remains to be done to reach all of Mozambique's population.

RELIGION

A 2007 census in Mozambique reported that about 19 percent of the population in Mozambique follows no religion. However, some scholars say that many of those who reported having no faith actually practice one of the many African traditional religions. Most African traditional religions are based on the belief that spirits exist in everything in nature—people, animals, plants, and even stones. Traditional observances may include the worship of ancestors and the practice of ancient rituals.

A Muslim mosque, or place of worship, in Inhambane. According to the 2007, about 4.1 million Mozambicans (approximately 18 percent of the total population) are Muslims.

The Islamic faith first came to Mozambique during the eighth century, brought to the eastern coast by Arab traders. Today, about 18 percent of Mozambicans are Muslim. Most of them live in the northern part of the country.

The indigenous people of Mozambique were exposed to Christianity by European missionaries beginning in the 16th century. Today, large populations of Protestant and Catholics can be found in the country, mostly in the southern region. Many Mozambicans combine their Christian beliefs with the dances, chants, and rituals of African traditional religions.

About 28 percent of the population of Mozambique belongs to the Roman Catholic Church, which is the largest Christian denomination in the country. Three archdioceses have been established in the cities of Maputo, Beira, and Nampula to serve the Catholic community.

The largest Protestant sect is the Zionist Christian Church, which accounts for 15.5 percent of the population. A variety of smaller Protestant groups are scattered throughout the country.

When Mozambique was a Portuguese colony, Christian holy days were national holidays. But after gaining independence in 1975, the country no longer recognized the religious holidays of Muslims or Christians. For the most part, national holidays reflect important dates in Mozambique's recent history.

(Opposite) A city of high-rises and out-door markets, the urban center of Maputo boasts a population of more than a million residents. (Right) A man and boy urge their donkey forward on an unpaved country road. About 60 percent of Mozambique's population lives in rural areas.

6 Diverse Communities

ALTHOUGH MORE THAN HALF of Mozambique's people live in villages and rural areas, in recent years many have migrated to the cities, in search of jobs. Today about 40 percent of Mozambique's almost 20 million people live in urban areas.

Each city in Mozambique has its own flavor and contributes to the nation in its own way. Some cities are centuries old and feature old colonial-style architecture. Others are just a few decades old.

MAPUTO

Located in far southeastern Mozambique, on Maputo Bay (formerly Delagoa Bay), Mozambique's capital city was founded in 1780 by Portuguese settlers. They originally named the town Lourenço Marques, after the Portuguese trader who had explored the area in the 1500s. The city became the capital of Portuguese East Africa in 1907. After Mozambique achieved independence, in 1975, the city remained the nation's capital, but was renamed Maputo.

Today, Maputo is Mozambique's largest city, with more than 1 million residents. Another 500,000 live in the metropolitan area surrounding the city. Maputo serves not only as the nation's capital but also as its main port and most vibrant commercial center. Railways link the city to the nations of Zimbabwe, South Africa, and Swaziland. Among the many industries based in Maputo are food processing, petroleum refining, and the manufacture of footwear and clothing.

Public gardens, paved sidewalks decorated with mosaic tiles, and marble-fronted public buildings make Maputo an attractive tourist destination. Among the popular sites are the city's military and historical museums and its 18th-century Portuguese fortress. Maputo also boasts the nation's first university, the Eduardo Mondlane University, which was established in 1962.

Before Mozambique became independent, Maputo attracted many tourists, mostly from South Africa and Rhodesia. The city was known for its attractive, tree-lined streets and sandy beaches. However, during the 1970s the tourist industry in Mozambique was harmed by its ongoing civil strife, and the newly installed government did little to promote the industry. Since the mid-1990s, however, efforts to encourage visitors from other counties have produced a rise in tourism that has benefited the economy of Maputo.

BEIRA

Founded by the Portuguese in the early 1500s, the seaport city of Beira serves as the center of the country's commercial fishing industry. It is located on the eastern coast of Mozambique, at the mouth of the Pungwe River. Beira is Mozambique's second-largest city, with an estimated population of about

A view of downtown Beira, the second-largest city in Mozambique.

500,000. It serves as the capital of Sofala Province, a mountainous region that includes Gorongosa National Park, located north of the city.

One of Mozambique's most important port cities and trading centers, Beira is a bustling community filled with old buildings, modern cafes, and stunning beaches. Its railways link western Mozambique and the landlocked African nations of Malawi, Zimbabwe, and Zambia with vital access to trade by sea. Major industries in Beira include ship repair, cotton milling, food processing, and tourism.

NAMPULA

Located in the interior of Mozambique, Nampula is the country's third-largest city, with a population of more than 470,000. Unlike Maputo and Beira, Nampula is not a port city but a centrally located agricultural trade center. Rail lines connect the city with Malawi and to the seaport cities of Lumbo and Nacala.

Founded in 1967 by the Portuguese government, Nampula was created by draining swampland in an area midway between the farming communities around Lake Malawi and the coast. Many trading companies, banks, and other businesses maintain offices in Nampula. There is also a strong cement manufacturing industry.

TETE

The capital of the Tete Province, the city of Tete is located on a plateau about 500 meters above sea level, in western Mozambique. Located on the Zambezi River, Tete was founded in 1531 by the Portuguese. Like the nearby town of

A merchant in a Nampula market offers various fruits and vegetables for sale.

Sena, founded at the same time, Tete served as an important river port during Portuguese rule. Many trading and military expeditions bound for the interior stopped in these cities.

Today Tete is a major transportation hub and trade center, particularly for cotton and cattle. It also offers a variety of tourist attractions. One famous site is the Tete suspension bridge, built in the 1960s, which crosses the Zambezi River to link Tete with the city of Moatize. Tourists also often visit the nearby 19th-century Baroma Church and the Cahora Bassa Dam, for guided tours of the huge power station and fifth-largest dam in the world.

QUELIMANE

The capital city of Zambezia Province (the most-populous province of Mozambique), Quelimane lies on the Bons Sinais River, north of the Zambezi River. Originally founded as a Swahili trading center, the town was occupied by the Portuguese in 1544. During the 1700s and 1800s, the city served as a slave market. Quelimane gained fame in 1856 as the end point of Scottish missionary David Livingstone's three-year journey across Africa. (Livingstone was the first European to travel from the Atlantic Ocean east to the Indian Ocean.)

The ruins of San Sebastian Fortress, a 400-year-old Portuguese fort on Mozambique Island.

Today, around 190,000 people live in Quelimane. Exports such as sisal and tea pass through this important trade center, which is also a leader in Mozambique's fishing industry.

MOZAMBIQUE ISLAND

Located off the coast of the northern province of Nampula, the tiny island of Mozambique Island is the former administrative capital of Mozambique. It is also a unique place with a long, rich past. Like many of the country's other coastal communities, Mozambique Island was once a fortified Portuguese trading post that served ships enroute to India.

Some of the structures that stood in the late 1600s remain today, blending in with newer structures that have been built since. Mozambique Island is known for its unique architecture—many buildings are constructed of coral, although several have deteriorated or been abandoned over time. In 1991, much of Mozambique Island was declared a World Heritage Site by the United Nations Educational, Scientific and Cultural Organization (UNESCO). This designation should support funding efforts to conserve the community, including the rehabilitation of its famous San Sebastian Fortress.

A CALENDAR OF MOZAMBICAN FESTIVALS

Public holidays in Mozambique commemorate the country's recent history of revolt against Portugal, the leaders who helped bring about independence, and the people of Mozambique.

January

On January 1, family and friends join together to celebrate **New Year's Day**.

February

February 3 is **Heroes' Day**, which marks the day Eduardo Mondlane, founder of Frelimo, was assassinated by a mail bomb.

April

April 7 is **Women's Day**.

May

May 1 is **Worker's Day**, which is observed as a holiday in many countries around the world to honor labor movements and organizations. In 2005 the Mozambique government used this day to discuss HIV / AIDS awareness, because of the disease's impact on the working-age population.

June

On June 25, Mozambicans celebrate **Independence Day**. On this date in 1975, the nation achieved independence from Portugal. Mozambicans celebrate the day with parades and political rallies.

September

Lusaka Agreement Day (also known as **Victory Day**) falls on September 7. It commemorates the signing in 1974 of the Lusaka peace treaty between Portugal and Frelimo in which Mozambique was promised independence.

On September 25, people celebrate **Armed Forces Day** (also called **Revolution Day**). It commemorates the day in 1964 when Frelimo rebels first began fighting against Portuguese rule. Mozambicans remember this day as the beginning of their country's struggle to become independent.

October

October 4 is **Peace and Reconciliation Day.** During this feast day, people celebrate the day of the signing in 1992 of the Peace General Agreement that officially ended the civil war in Mozambique.

October 19 is **Samora Machel Day,** which honors the life of the Frelimo leader and first president of Mozambique. It is celebrated on the day of his death, which occurred when his plane crashed in South Africa.

A CALENDAR OF MOZAMBICAN FESTIVALS

November

Maputo City Day is celebrated on November 10 in the city of Maputo. It honors the capital city.

December

On December 25 the country celebrates **Family Day**.

Religious Observances

Mozambique's Muslims and Christians observe several holy days related to their religions. Some of these fall on specific days of each year; for example, **Christmas** (which celebrates the birth of Jesus Christ) is observed on December 25. Many other major celebrations occur according to the lunar calendar, in which the months correspond to the phases of the moon. A lunar month is shorter than a typical month of the Western calendar. Therefore, the festival dates vary from year to year. Other celebrations are observed seasonally.

A very important month of the Muslim lunar calendar is the ninth month, **Ramadan**. This is a time of sacrifice for devout Muslims. Mozambican Muslims celebrate **Eid al-Fitr** to mark the end of Ramadan. **Eid al-Adha** (Feast of the Sacrifice) takes place in the last month of the Muslim calendar during the **Hajj** period, when Muslims make a pilgrimage to Mecca. The holiday honors the prophet Abraham, who was willing to sacrifice his own son to Allah. Each of these holidays is celebrated with a feast. On **Eid al-Adha**, families traditionally eat a third of the feast and donate the rest to the poor.

The major Christian festivals on the lunar cycle involve the suffering and death of Jesus Christ. **Ash Wednesday** marks the start of a period of self-sacrifice called **Lent**, which lasts for 40 days. The final eight days of Lent are known as **Holy Week**. A number of important days are observed, including **Palm Sunday**, which commemorates Jesus' arrival in Jerusalem; **Holy Thursday**, which marks the night of the last Supper; **Good Friday**, the day of Jesus' death on the cross; and **Easter Monday**, which marks his resurrection. (In Western countries, **Easter** is typically celebrated on the day before.)

RECIPES

Frango A Cafrial (Barbecued Chicken)

(Serves 8)
4 2-1/2 lb. chickens
1 Tbsp. salt
1 tsp. garlic powder
1 tsp. paprika
1/2 tsp. ground ginger
1/2 tsp. cayenne pepper
1/2 cup salad oil

Directions:

1. Combine spices and salad oil in a bowl. Rub each of the chickens with the spice mixture, coating all sides thoroughly.
2. Roast the chickens uncovered in a 375° F oven for 1-1/4 to 1-1/2 hours or until the meat is no longer pink. Baste the chickens occasionally with the seasoned oil during roasting.
3. Cut the chickens in half. Serve with 1 cup cooked rice per person.

Piri-Piri (Hot Pepper)

4 Tbsp. coarse red pepper
1 Tbsp. salt
1 tsp. garlic powder
1 Tbsp. lemon juice
4 Tbsp. olive oil

Directions:

1. Combine all the ingredients in a small bowl. Use this hot pepper sparingly as a spice; amount used depends on personal taste.

Sopa De Feijao Verde (String Bean Soup)

(Serves 8)

1 1/2 quarts of water
1 cup instant potatoes
1 6-oz. can tomato sauce
1 Tbsp. onion powder
1 package frozen Italian green beans, thawed and cut into thin slices

Directions:

1. Bring the water to a boil in a 3-quart saucepan.
2. Add all the ingredients to the water and simmer for about 10 minutes, or until the beans are tender.

Salada Pera De Abacate (Avocado Salad)

(Serves 8)

1 head iceberg lettuce
2 tomatoes
2 avocados

Directions:

1. Cut the lettuce into 3/4-inch thick, round slices and place each slice on a plate.
2. Cut each tomato and each avocado into eight pieces. Alternate tomato slices and avocado slices on top of lettuce, using two tomato slices and two avocado slices on each salad.
3. Drizzle 2 tablespoons of lemon dressing on top of each serving.

Rabanadas de Pao (Portuguese Sweet Toast)

(Serves 4 to 6)

1 loaf of unsliced bread
2 eggs
13 Tbsp. of milk
cooking oil (enough to coat inside of frying pan)
1/2 cup sugar
2 tsp. ground cinnamon

Directions:
1. Mix sugar and cinnamon in small bowl and set aside.
2. Cut the loaf of bread into thick slices.
3. In a bowl, beat eggs and mix with milk. Dip each slice of bread in the egg/milk mixture and then fry in hot cooking oil in a frying pan until the slice browns on each side.
4. Remove from the frying pan, and sprinkle each side with the sugar/cinnamon mixture before serving.

Lemon Dressing (For Avocado Salad)

(Serves 8)

1 cup lemon juice
1 cup olive oil
1 cup peach syrup
1 tsp. salad herbs
1 tsp. salt
1/4 tsp. pepper

Directions:
1. Combine the lemon juice and olive oil in a jar. Add syrup, salad herbs, salt, and pepper to the lemon juice/olive oil mixture. Shake well.
2. Drizzle 2 tablespoons of dressing onto each serving of Avocado Salad.

Delicias De Mel (Honey Delight)

(Serves 12)

4 eggs
2 cups sugar
4 Tbsp. honey
2 Tbsp. melted butter
2 cups milk
3 cups flour
2 tsp. baking powder
2 tsp. cinnamon

Directions:
1. Separate the egg yolks and egg whites. Mix the egg yolks with the sugar and melted butter. Add the remaining ingredients, except for the egg whites.
2. In a separate bowl, beat the egg whites until they become creamy and thick. Then add the beaten egg whites to the rest of the mixture.
3. Pour the mixture into a buttered and floured baking pan. Bake at 350 degrees until the mixture turns golden brown.

GLOSSARY

archipelago—a group of islands.

cassava—a plant whose starchy root is a major food source in Africa.

city-state—an independent city that has its own government and controls the lands surrounding it.

colonize—to establish a settlement with economic and political ties to the home country.

concession—granting of land in return for specified services.

decolonization—the process of freeing a colony from colonial status.

ecotourism—tourism that addresses environmental concerns, such as wildlife and habitat preservation, as well as social concerns, such as providing economic benefits to local communities.

ethnic group—people of the same racial background who share a common culture or tradition.

gross domestic product (GDP)—the total value of goods and services produced by a country in a single year.

habitat—the place in which a plant or animal naturally lives.

indigenous—originating in or native to a particular area.

infrastructure—basic facilities and services that may include roads, railways, bridges; water supplies; and electrical power generation.

International Monetary Fund—an organization of 184 countries whose goals are to reduce poverty, promote employment, help increase international trade, and promote economic growth of poor countries.

plateau—a level area of land.

poach—illegally kill, capture, or collect wildlife.

sanction—an economic or military measure placed on a nation by a group of countries in an effort to bring about policy change.

savanna—dry, open grasslands with scattered trees.

smelter—a processing plant where ore is melted so that metals can be separated.

socialist—an economic system in which the production of goods by businesses, factories, and farms is controlled by the government.

tropics—region near the equator where the climate is warm enough to support plant growth year-round.

unicameral—having a single-chamber legislature.

PROJECT AND REPORT IDEAS

Maps

Draw a map that shows the geography of Mozambique. It should include the following features: the Indian Ocean, the Lebombo Mountains, the Rovuma and Zambezi Rivers, Maputo Bay, the capital city of Maputo, the Mozambique Channel, the Inyanga Mountains, Monte Binge, Serra Da Gorongosa, and Lakes Nyasa and Cahora Bassa.

Research and draw a map illustrating that route that Vasco da Gama took, beginning in 1497, from Portugal to India. Identify the following on your map: Portugal, Mozambique, India, and the Cape of Good Hope. Also include the dates when da Gama reached various locations.

The Flag and Its Symbolism

Research the flag of Mozambique. Draw and color a picture of the flag, and write a report to accompany it. Your report should include when the flag was adopted and what its colors symbolize.

Historical Timeline

Create a timeline of Mozambican history. Begin your timeline with the arrival of the Bantu speakers around the first century A.D. and end with a recent, major political event involving Mozambique that you find in a newspaper story, newsmagazine article, or on the Internet.

Mozambique's Political Structure

Create a chart detailing Mozambique's three branches of government. Include the names of the president and prime minister and the parties represented in the legislature.

Cyclone Eline

Find information in newspapers, magazines, and on the Internet about Cyclone Eline and the destruction it caused in Mozambique. Write a report about what you learned. Be sure to answer the following questions in your report: When did Cyclone Eline hit? Was there any warning? What kind of destruction did the storm cause? Which countries or international organizations stepped forward to help Mozambique recover? What has the lasting impact been?

CHRONOLOGY

ca. 1300 B.C.: Ancestors of the Khoisan people begin forming organized tribes.

First century A.D.: Bantu-speaking people come to the area.

ca. A.D. 800: Arabs and small groups of Swahili traders settle along the Indian Ocean coast.

1498: Portuguese explorer Vasco da Gama stops at the African trading centers of Inhambane and Moçambique on his way to India.

1505: The Portuguese begin colonizing the area.

1600s to 1800s: Portuguese landowners known as *prazeros* control vast estates run by forced labor.

1880: The Portuguese government revokes the land claims of the *prazeros*.

1961: Eduardo Mondlane forms the guerrilla group The Front for the Liberation of Mozambique (Frelimo) to fight against Portuguese rule in Mozambique.

1964: Frelimo rebels attack the Mozambique government and win control of the northern part of the country.

1975: Mozambique gains independence from Portugal; Frelimo leader Samora Machel is named the country's first president.

1976: Cahora Bassa power plant opens near Tete.

1980s: Fighting breaks out between Frelimo and a rebel group called the Mozambican National Resistance (Renamo).

1986: President Samora Machel is killed in a plane crash; he is succeeded by Joaquim Chissano.

1990: A constitution establishing a democratic republic in Mozambique is approved.

1992: Frelimo and Renamo sign a peace treaty, ending the 16-year civil war.

CHRONOLOGY

1994:   The first free elections are held; Joaquim Chissano is elected president.

2000:   Cyclone Eline and heavy rains batter the southern provinces, causing deadly floods.

2001:   Additional flooding devastates southern Mozambique.

2004:   Armando Guebuza is elected president.

2005:   Guebuza takes office in February; Luisa Diogo becomes the country's first female prime minister.

2006:   Mozambique assumes majority ownership of Cahora Bassa power plant; The World Bank approves $37 billion in debt relief.

2007:   Flooding along the Zambezi and Buzi Rivers force nearly 200,000 people to leave their homes and live in refugee camps for several months.

2008:   Mozambique's agriculture minister requests food aid from the United Nations because of drought and an acute food shortage.

2009:   Guebuza re-elected in a landslide victory marred by allegations of voter fraud; Frelimo party gains a 75% control over the Assembly.

2010:   Former minister Antonio Munguambe sentenced to 20 years in prison for embezzlement in the highest-level corruption conviction since 1975.

2012:   A substantial reserve of natural gas is discovered off the coast of Mozambique.

FURTHER READING/INTERNET RESOURCES

Fitzpatrick, Mary. *Lonely Planet Mozambique*. Melbourne, Aus.: Lonely Planet Publications, 2010.

Hanlon, Joseph. *Do Bicycles Equal Development in Mozambique?* Oxford: James Currey, 2010

King, David C. *Mozambique* (Cultures of the World). Salt Lake City: Benchmark Books, 2001

Minter, William. *Apartheid's Contras: An Inquiry into the Roots of War in Angola and Mozambique*. Charleston: Booksurge Publishing, 2008.

Ndege, George. *Culture and Customs of Mozambique*. Westport, CT: Greenwood, 2006.

History and Geography

http://www.state.gov/r/pa/ei/bgn/7035.htm
http://www.africa.com/mozambique
http://kids.yahoo.com/reference/world-factbook/country/mz—Mozambique

Economic and Political Information

https://www.cia.gov/library/publications/the-world-factbook/geos/mz.html
http://maputo.usembassy.gov/
http://news.bbc.co.uk/2/hi/europe/country_profiles/1063120.stm

Culture and Festivals

http://www.mapsofworld.com/mozambique/culture/
http://www.everyculture.com/Ma-Ni/Mozambique.html
http://kadmusarts.com/countries/Mozambique.html

Travel Information

http://www.lonelyplanet.com/mozambique
http://www.world66.com/africa/mozambique
http://travel.state.gov/travel/cis_pa_tw/cis/cis_976.html

FOR MORE INFORMATION

U.S. Embassy in Mozambique
Av. Kenneth Kaunda, 193
Maputo, Mozambique
Caixa Postal, 783
Tel: (258) 21-49 27 97
Fax:(258) 21-49 01 14
E-mail: maputoirc@state.gov
Website: http://maputo.usembassy.gov

Embassy of the Republic of Mozambique
1525 New Hampshire Avenue, NW
Washington, DC 20036
Tel: (202) 293-7146
Fax: (202) 835-0245
E-mail: embamoc@aol.com
Website: http://www.embamoc-usa.org

U.S. Department of State
Bureau of Consular Affairs
2100 Pennsylvania Ave. NW, 4th Floor
Washington, DC 20037
Tel: (202) 736 9130

INDEX

Numbers in **bold italic** refer to captions.

CONTRIBUTORS/PICTURE CREDITS

Professor Robert I. Rotberg is Director of the Program on Intrastate Conflict and Conflict Resolution at the Kennedy School, Harvard University, and President of the World Peace Foundation. He is the author of a number of books and articles on Africa, including *A Political History of Tropical Africa* and *Ending Autocracy, Enabling Democracy: The Tribulations of Southern Africa.*

Tanya Mulroy earned a bachelor's degree in special education from Moorhead State University in Moorhead, Minnesota. She worked as a special education teacher in Massachusetts. She now spends her days writing and enjoying her family at their home in Boston, Massachusetts.